For adventurers who are reluctant,
adventurers who are enthusiastic
and for adventurers who are reluctant
and then become enthusiastic.

With thanks to Ben (my adventure buddy), Emily
and the team at Tundra.

Text and illustrations copyright © 2019 by Madeline Kloepper

Tundra Books, an imprint of Penguin Random House Canada Young Readers,
a Penguin Random House Company

Library and Archives Canada Cataloguing in Publication

Kloepper, Madeline, author
      The not-so great outdoors / Madeline Kloepper.

Issued in print and electronic formats.
ISBN 978-0-7352-6417-5 (hardcover).—ISBN 978-0-7352-6418-2 (ebook) —
ISBN 978-0-7352-6898-2 (special markets)

      I. Title.

PS8621.L637N68 2019   jC813'.6   C2018-902940-4
                                               C2018-902960-9

Published simultaneously in the United States of America by Tundra Books
of Northern New York, an imprint of Penguin Random House Canada Young
Readers, a Penguin Random House Company

Library of Congress Control Number 2018946081

Acquired by Tara Walker
Edited by Jessica Burgess
Designed by John Martz
The artwork in this book was rendered in mixed media
and finished digitally.
The text was set in Icone.

Printed and bound in China

www.penguinrandomhouse.ca

1   2   3   4   5   24   23   22   21   20

Penguin
Random House
tundra   TUNDRA BOOKS

The NOT-SO Great Outdoors

by Madeline Kloepper

tundra

I have no idea why we have to "venture into the great outdoors" this summer . . .

It's not like there's anything out here.

There's no electricity.

There are no fountains
or sculptures.

There aren't even any *playgrounds*!

I can't look out my window
at the city lights.

And where does
anything live?

It's not like there are
any buildings.

And I can't walk through the dog park
on my way home from school.

Although *something* smells
like wet dog . . .

We should probably go home now.

Liam couldn't possibly go another
night without his teddy . . .

. . . bears?!

Well, I guess I could get by with songbirds
instead of street performers.

And I suppose catching a bus doesn't
exactly compare to catching a fish.

The construction workers here *are* pretty good at rerouting traffic.

Especially since the roads can get a bit bumpy.

And the skyline isn't too shabby.

I wonder if that new restaurant
downtown knows how good *this* tastes?

I don't even mind that
I'm missing my favorite show.

So maybe it's all right to spend time with the herd . . .

Especially when
the outdoors can be so great!